close up

frank b. edwards & laurel aziz

bungalo books

microscopic photographs of everyday stuff

**Written by Frank B. Edwards and
Laurel Aziz**
Copyright 1992 by Bungalo Books

**Canadian Cataloguing in Publication
Data**

Edwards, Frank B., 1952-
   Close up: microscopic photographs
   of everyday stuff

ISBN 0-921285-25-6 (bound)
ISBN 0-921285-24-8 (pbk.)

I. Photomicrography — Juvenile Literature.
I. Aziz, Laurel, 1956-
II. Title.

QH278.E49 1992   j578.'4   C92-090403-3

Published in Canada by:
Bungalo Books
Box 129
Newburgh, Ontario
KOK 2S0

Co-published in U.S.A. by:
Firefly Books (U.S.) Inc.
Ellicott Station
P.O. Box 1338
Buffalo, New York
14205

Trade Distribution:
Firefly Books Ltd.
250 Sparks Avenue
Willowdale, Ontario
M2H 2S4

Designed by:
Linda J. Menyes

Printed in Canada by:
Friesen Printers
Altona, Manitoba

Film preparation by:
Hadwen Graphics
Ottawa, Ontario

contents

Grains of salt and sugar are hard to tell apart with the naked eye. But a photograph from a scanning electron microscope (SEM), facing page, enlarged 71 times, makes it easy to distinguish them. Salt crystals are small and six-sided, while sugar crystals are larger and darker and

have 10 sides. Brown sugar, left, is less refined than white, and its crystals tend to stay lumped together.

Optical microscopes use glass lenses to enlarge specimens up to 2,000 times, while the SEM can enlarge its subjects by one million times their normal size. Using magnetic instead of glass lenses, the SEM creates an image by bombarding the specimen with electrons. When these electrons bounce off the specimen, they pass through a magnetic "lens" to a projector that sends a signal to a television screen. The final image, which can be photographed, depicts the shape and texture of the object that the electrons hit. (Facing page magnified 71 times. Left magnified 33 times.)

Although the mosquito's compound eyes are large, they are not the primary tool used to find her next victim. Instead, she relies on the sensory hairs and antennae that cover her slender body to alert her to warmth, moisture and carbon dioxide, the chemical cues emitted by warm-blooded prey.

Egg-laying females need a high-protein diet, so they do most of the biting in the mosquito family. Extending downward from the base of the head is a long, feathery feeding tube, called the proboscis, a lower lip that houses the needle-sharp lancets which puncture the skin of the victim when the proboscis tip makes contact. (The male's similarly shaped mouthparts are less effective at piercing skin, and they feed mostly on sap they siphon from plants.)

Once the flesh is torn, pumps in the mosquito's head and thorax silently suck blood upward. At the same time, tiny glands contained in the thorax spit out a saliva that combats the victim's natural clotting response to openings in the skin. It is this injection of blood-thinning saliva, however, that leaves the itchy reminder of the mosquito's visit.

An unmistakable whine usually forewarns human victims of a mosquito attack — a droning alarm produced by its wings as they beat 300 to 500 times per second. (Magnified 163 times.)

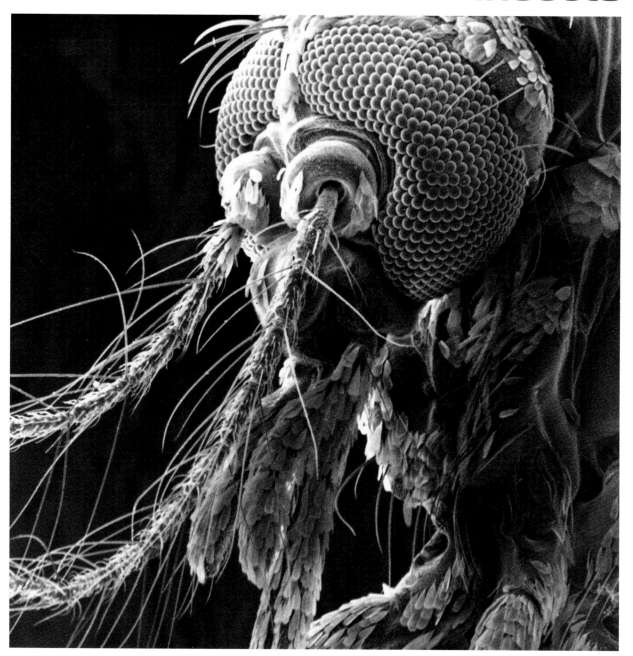

While some species of spiders simply spin a web and wait for their prey, spiders that hunt must track their victims and rely much more on their eyes. Most spiders have eight simple eyes, and their placement varies with the species. The strongest eyes for forming an image are the main, or anterior median, eyes, centred on the spider's face, right. Outwardly positioned secondary eyes provide peripheral vision, and a row located on the bottom measures distance or detects motion within a narrow field of view.

Instead of antennae, spiders have an array of bristly sense organs called spines on their eight legs; their bodies are also covered with short, fine hairs, or setae, that are sensitive to touch, temperature and chemical signals.

Whether a hunter or a sit-and-wait trapper, a spider uses the mandibles under its bottom row of eyes for carrying, digging and catching prey. Since a spider lacks teeth, it injects its prey with a powerful saliva, dissolving the victim into a nutritious drink that is slurped up through a tube called the prebuccal cavity. The indigestible exterior is discarded. (Magnified 82 times.)

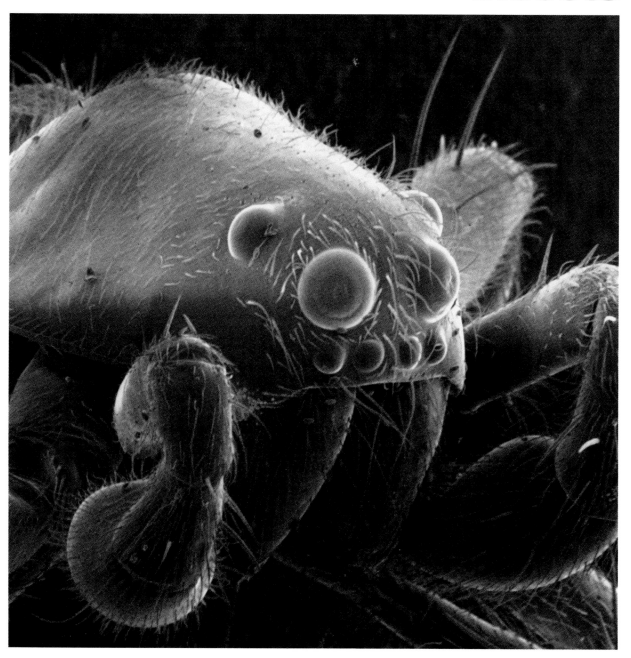

 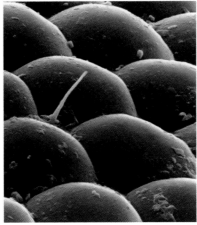

The highly manoeuvrable house-fly, *Musca domestica*, relies on its excellent vision for precision flying and landing. A large portion of its head is taken up by compound eyes, above left, which offer a wide field of vision. Such eyes are highly sensitive to movement because of the numerous facets available to receive light impulses. But big eyes are not necessarily better. The fly's vision is neither particularly sharp nor good at a distance, since the eyes do not move within the sockets and cannot be focused. To see an object more clearly, the fly must move closer to it.

While the compound eye is made up of hundreds of lenses, above right, it does not see multiple images, as we can see, for example, a wall of 100 television screens all set to the same channel. Rather, each of the complete and separately functioning eye elements takes in only a slice of the overall visual field. The separate parts of the picture are transmitted to photoreceptors near the base of the pyramid-shaped lens, where the overall image is tied together. Hairs found above the eye, facing page, work like our eyelashes to reduce the glare from any light shining over the fly's lenses. (Above left magnified 29 times. Above right magnified 453 times. Facing page magnified 730 times.)

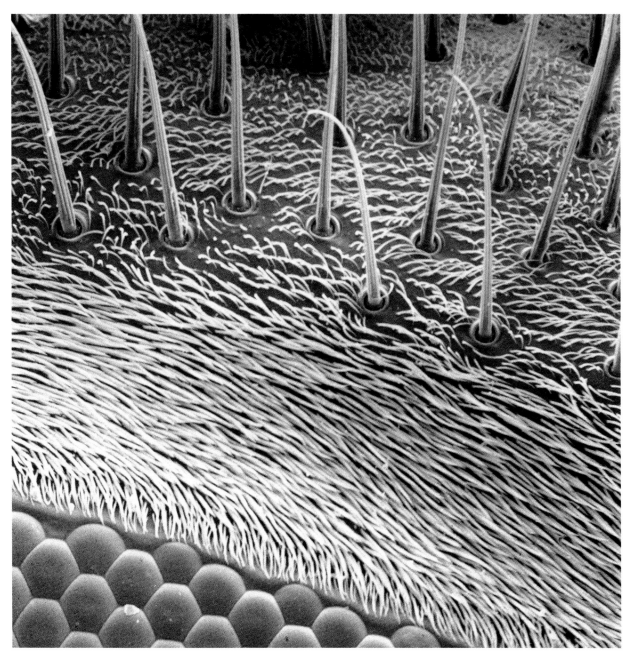

Its love of pets drives humans to distraction.

The adult cat flea is marvellously adapted to its life in the coat of its mammalian host. A rounded head cap, vertically tapered body and backward-facing spines allow this parasitic insect to weave effortlessly through the thick fur standing in its path. The comblike spines, called ctenidia, also help keep the flea securely anchored, despite the best efforts of both cat and owner to remove it.

Fleas belong to the family of insects known as Siphonaptera. *Siphon* refers to the flea's blood-sucking habit, a behaviour that causes multiple and annoying bites. And while *apteros* may mean wingless, the mobility of *ctenocephalides felis* is not at all impaired by the absence of flight. Propelled by long, multi-jointed legs, this species is remarkably skilled at leaping from host to host. Despite its small size, the cat flea has recorded incredible jumps of more than 100 times its body length. A comparable single bound by a human athlete would measure the length of two football fields. (Magnified 522 times.)

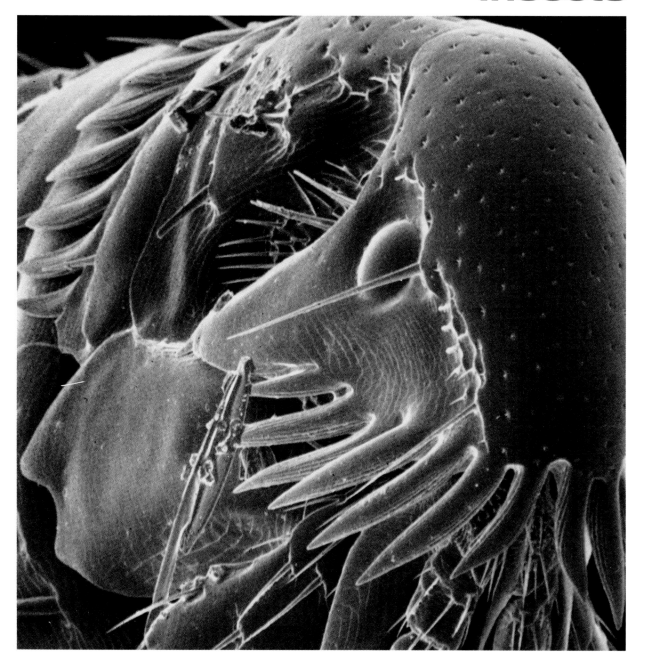

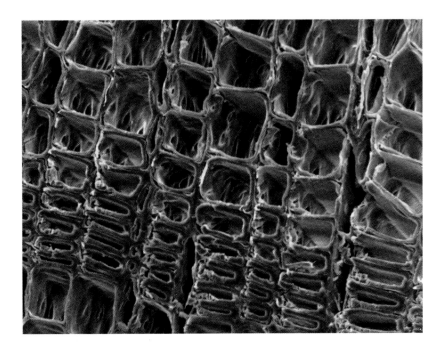

The events of a tree's life are recorded in its growth rings. Regular, evenly spaced rings, shown in a cross section of cedar, facing page, bear testimony to an uneventful life in which each year's new growth is about the same as the others.

Growth rings vary according to the size of their individual cells, above. In the lush spring growing season, the tree produces large-diameter cells, called tracheids, in its new sapwood to accommodate the supply of nutrients rushing up from the roots. But during the summer, when the year's new cell growth slows and eventually comes to a halt, the diameter of these cells decreases dramatically, and they appear squashed between the larger spring cells on either side. Each band of small cells marks that year's new growth and indicates the tree's age.

The new tracheids function as arteries for several years, carrying nutrients from the roots up to the branches. But gradually, the old tissue fills up with oils, gums and resins and finally becomes part of the solid heartwood that gives a tree its structural strength. (Above magnified 568 times. Facing page magnified 313 times.)

**Delivered
by insects,
this grain
is essential
to the next
generation.**

A pollen grain from a daisy, facing page, resembles a stylized meteorite, a shape that is part of nature's intriguing "lock and key" fertilization system. In order to prevent genetic confusion, nature has given each plant's pollen a unique shape to ensure that it pollinates a member of the correct species.

Formed in the anther, or male part of the flower, daisy pollen grains are usually transported to the female portion of neighbouring plants by insects. The exterior of each pollen grain, which is covered with a durable coat capable of resisting acids and extreme heat during its travels, is studded so that it will fasten itself firmly upon the sticky stigma of the flower.

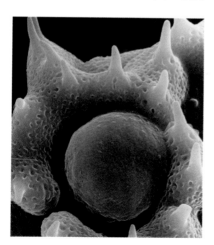

Once the pollen grain arrives at its destination, the fertilization process begins. The round opening on the grain, left, called an operculum, covers the spore-bearing part of the pollen. When the pollen contacts the stigma, it germinates and sends a pollen tube down into the flower's embryo sac. There, it will release sperm cells that will fuse with female cells to form an embryo. (Facing page magnified 4,500 times. Left magnified 4,500 times.)

Designed to attract, this surface smells as good as it looks.

Resembling a gently rolling landscape, cells on the surface of a daisy petal, facing page, give it a velvety softness. Swollen from the sap and water flowing through its vascular system, the petal's ridged surface contains deposits of colourful pigments and glands that release fragrances to attract the attention of insect pollinators.

The rounded cellular mounds are, in fact, somewhat irregularly arranged hexagons, right. The six-sided figure is very common in nature because it is the most efficient shape for fitting the maximum number of

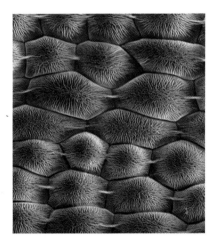

cells into the minimum amount of available space. (Above magnified 366 times. Facing page magnified 2,650 times.)

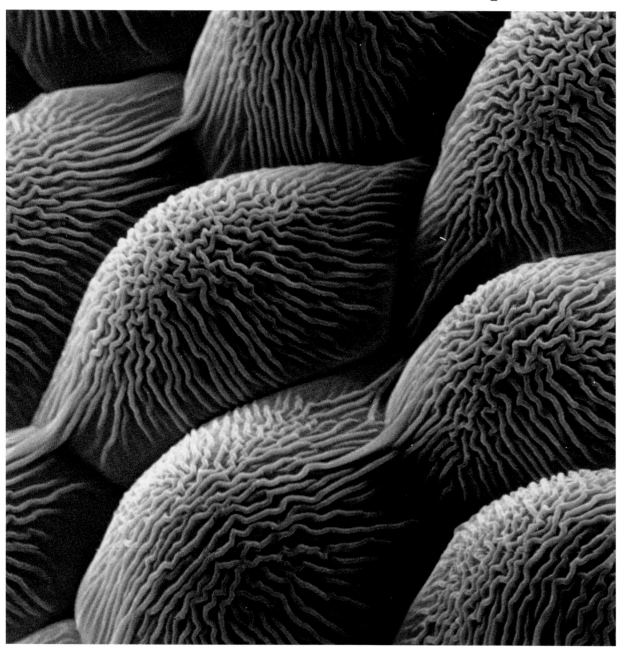

An explosive favourite, this snack food offers more taste than substance.

Aptly named from the Middle English word *poppe*, which means an explosive sound, a kernel of popcorn bursts into an elaborate honeycomblike structure of fluffed starch when heated. This variety of corn, known as maize, "explodes" because of a special ingredient: water. As a kernel cooks, the water it contains is heated. When the water is converted to steam, it expands and cooks the surrounding starch molecules, which are forced outward through the skin. Once the vapour clears, however, only air is left to fill the spaces.

The custom of popping corn originated more than 5,000 years ago among native North Americans. As recently as the early 1900s, popcorn was sold by the sackful, cob and all, for roasting whole over an open fire. Today, the tradition is alive and well with at least 100,000 tons of the dynamic snack filling pots and microwave ovens across North America each year — an average of four large bowls per person. (Magnified 204 times.)

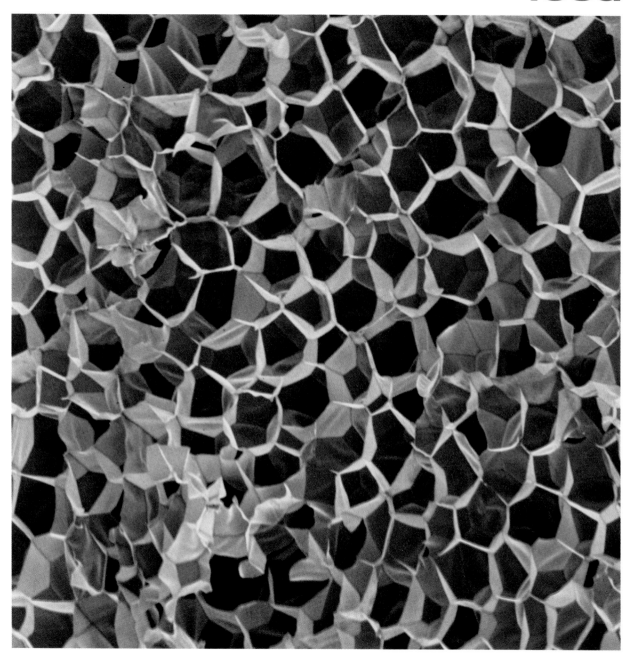

**A tangle of
soft spines
hides the
sweet nature
of this fruit.**

Covered with soft brown hairs, the skin of an unripened kiwifruit, right, looks like a tangled miniature forest. By the time the egg-shaped fruit is ready to eat, however, it will shed its downy coat.

The kiwifruit belongs to the family of Chinese gooseberries. Long before it was familiar to Western palates, *Actinidia chinensis* was canned, pickled and eaten fresh in China, where some 200,000 tons of it are still harvested annually from wild crops.

In 1904, the once-untamed delicacy of rural China (known as *yang-tao*) was introduced to New Zealand for commercial planting and given the name kiwifruit. (Magnified 169 times.)

22

These sweet air bubbles melt in your mouth.

The fact that sponge toffee is a mass of candied air bubbles helps to explain why it melts so quickly in the mouth.

Made from pure sugar in its liquid form, the candy begins as a gummy syrup that is boiled and mixed until it reaches a hard, brittle state. As the syrup heats, gas bubbles appear. Much lighter than the thickening syrup, however, the bubbles clump together and float upward as the toffee cools.

The slight tingling sensation you feel when sponge toffee touches your tongue is the result of a small amount of sodium bicarbonate (baking soda) that is added to the syrup during the cooking process. (Magnified 169 times.)

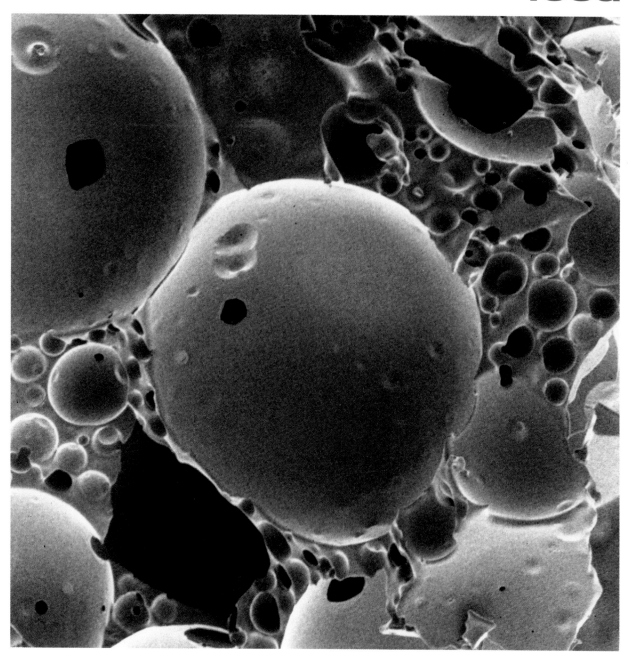

There is not a lot of fibre left in this soft white stuff.

The spherical globules suspended in bread crust, right, are carbohydrate molecules known as starch. Wheat, the principal cereal grain used in the production of bread in the Western world, is high in starchy carbohydrates, which make up almost three-quarters of the content of each grain.

Most of this naturally occurring starch is found layered in the grain's cell walls, but when the wheat kernels are milled into flour, their starch content is reduced to an odourless and tasteless powder. The addition of water during the preparation of bread dough reconstitutes the starch granules, so they gelatinize — rather than stiffen — during baking, giving the bread a soft and spongy texture. (Magnified 2,100 times.)

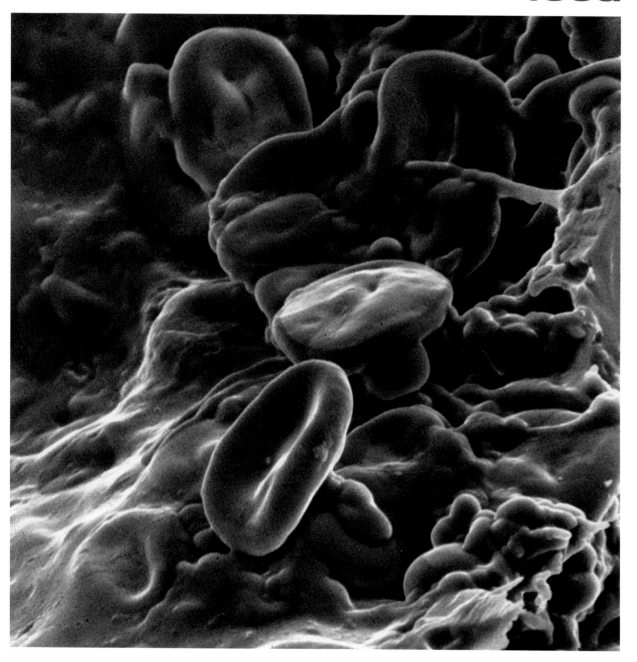

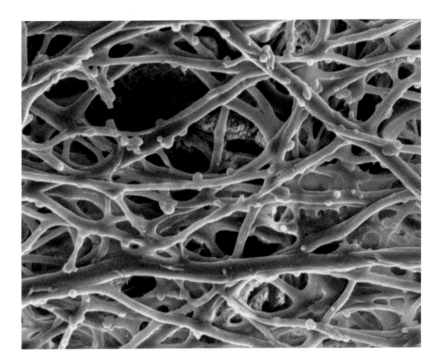

An eggshell, facing page, not only protects the embryo but also allows it to breathe and helps develop its skeleton.

The hard shell bears a striking resemblance to a rock cut in a limestone quarry. Like limestone, the shell is made up primarily of calcium carbonate, a substance also found in animal bones and snail shells. As the bird grows, its bones draw some calcium from the shell.

The inner layer of shell consists of a collection of calcite knobs which anchor the membrane, above, that surrounds the embryo. The membrane is actually a network of flattened protein fibres with pores that allow the embryo to breathe. The bases of the shell's calcite knobs form a smooth, porous outer wall that permits the vital exchange of oxygen and carbon dioxide. (Facing page magnified 347 times. Above magnified 710 times.)

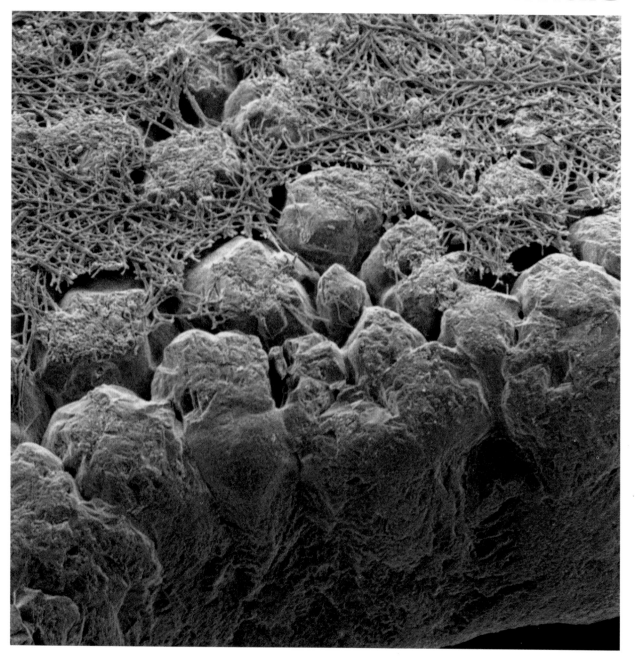

While ticklish to some, this material is necessary for the survival of its owner.

The texture of a rock dove feather, right, is as evenly woven as a loomed fabric. Durable filaments of a protein called keratin are closely spaced along the hollow shaft, or rachis. The naked eye sees these filaments, or barbs, as simple hairs, but both sides of each barb are actually lined with hundreds of individual hooked barbules that interlock with neighbouring ones, facing page, to align the feather filaments in a tight web. Such a secure hold gives each contour feather the airtight surface it needs for flight. Found only on birds, feathers are light for flight and vital to survival: they insulate

against the heat of the sun and the cold of winter and repel both rain and snow. (Above magnified 23 times. Facing page magnified 410 times.)

This tiny filter puts blood against water so that life can go on.

Framed in crescent-shaped, bony arches, the gills of the trout fingerling are its secret to underwater survival.

Humans obtain their oxygen supply from the air that surrounds them, drawing it in through the blood-rich sacs of their lungs as they breathe. Fish, likewise, are surrounded by oxygen, but it is dissolved in their watery habitat. To extract the precious gas, a fish must filter the oxygen from the water that it pumps across the neatly layered filaments lining the gill frames. Each of the thin-skinned filaments is loaded to the brim with a network of blood vessels, perfect for absorbing oxygen. As oxygen is taken in, carbon dioxide and wastes are simultaneously released. Typically, fish can absorb almost three-quarters of the oxygen present in the water that they push past their gills — a fast and efficient means of respiration. (Magnified 225 times.)

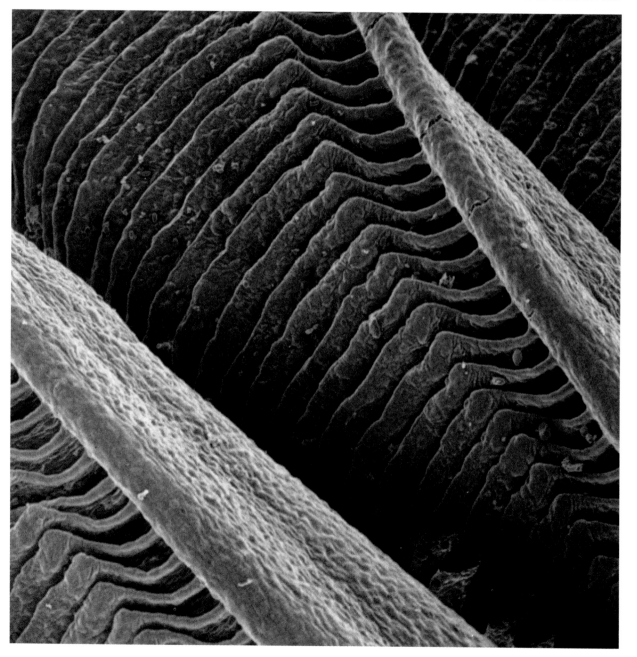

**Loaded
with genetic
information,
these cells
can trigger a
new life.**

Sperm cells from a mating bull, right, provide one-half of the genetic material needed to create a baby calf. When a male's sperm cell comes in contact with a cow's egg, they combine with one another to create a cell called a zygote that will develop into an embryo within the mother's womb. Known as germ cells, the sperm and egg do much more than simply create a new life — they also combine the genetic material of both parents, so the baby calf will have many of its parents' physical and mental traits.

The two distinguishable parts of the bovine sperm are its circular head and its long tail, which whips back and forth to move the sperm through the passageways that lead it to the female's immobile egg. The head is covered with a chemical substance that allows the sperm to penetrate the egg wall; then the nucleus inside the circular cap attaches itself to the egg. Inside the nucleus are 30 chromosomes, half the genetic information the zygote needs to begin the complicated task of developing into a healthy calf. The other 30 necessary chromosomes are contained in the mother's egg cell. (Magnified 8,170 times.)

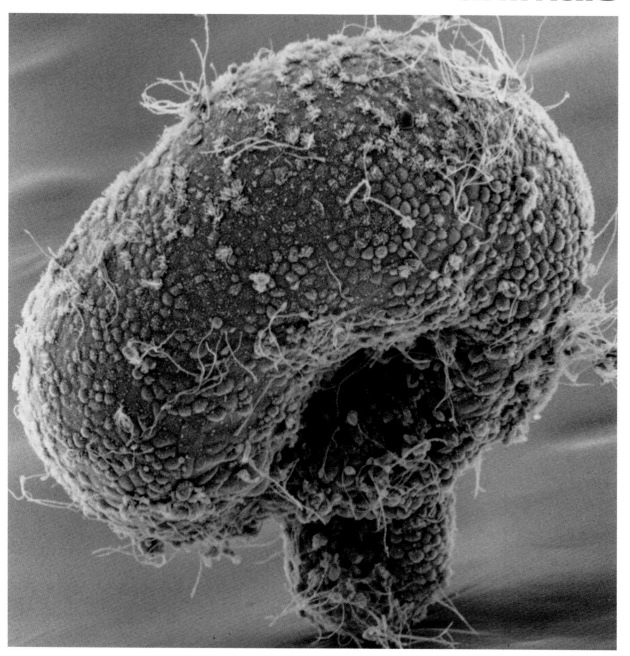

The outside wall props the bird up; the canals inside give it life.

Chicken bones have functions beyond providing diners with a handy grip during a finger-licking meal. In concert with each other, they make up the light skeleton that gives a chicken its gravity-defying shape and allows movement of its limbs.

But bones have two other important functions as well. They provide a reservoir of calcium that can be distributed to the body as needed (for the creation of eggshells, for example) and also house the blood-manufacturing system.

Within their rigid exterior walls, bones contain spongy canals filled with soft tissue called marrow. Early in the chicken's life, the bones' canals are filled with red marrow that produces the red blood cells that are necessary for healthy development. As the body matures, it needs fewer new blood cells, so much of the bone's tissue reverts to its structural duties and turns to yellow marrow, which is made up primarily of fat cells. (Magnified 522 times.)

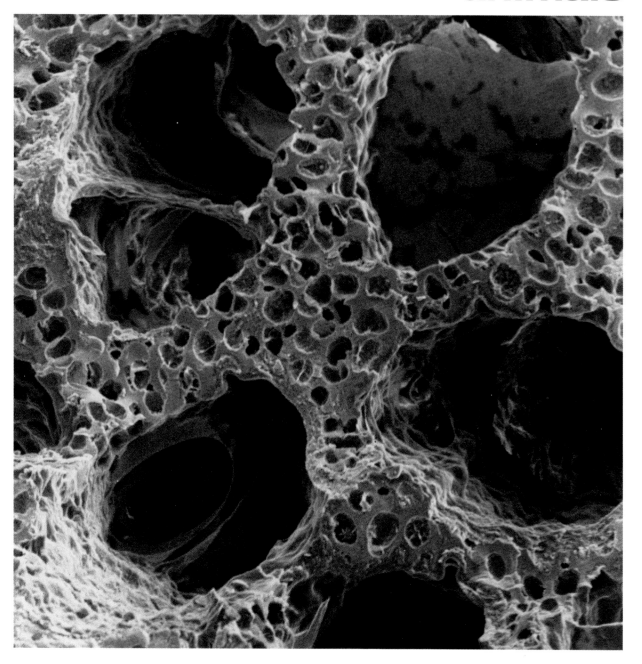

Strands of matted fibre, facing page, are clearly visible in a coarse brown paper towel — the kind found in most school washrooms. Paper is good towel material, since it can absorb a lot of moisture and is quite strong. This is because paper is made from cellulose, a tough fibre found in such plants as wood, cotton and straw that can hold lots of water.

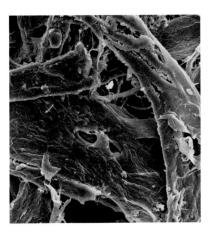

While writing paper is made with finely ground cellulose fibres that have been bleached white, cheap paper towels are made of larger fibres, below, that are left their natural colour. The fibres come from wood-chips or other materials with lots of cellulose that are broken down into individual fibres with heat and chemicals. When wet, the fibres absorb water and expand, but after a light beating, the pulpy solution is drained and pressed under rollers.

As the fibres lose their moisture in the process, they shrink and bind to one another, creating a strong paper. The paper remains strong only until it is used to soak up water or other liquids — then the fibres expand once more, lose their strength and turn to mush. (Facing page magnified 300 times. Left magnified 730 times.)

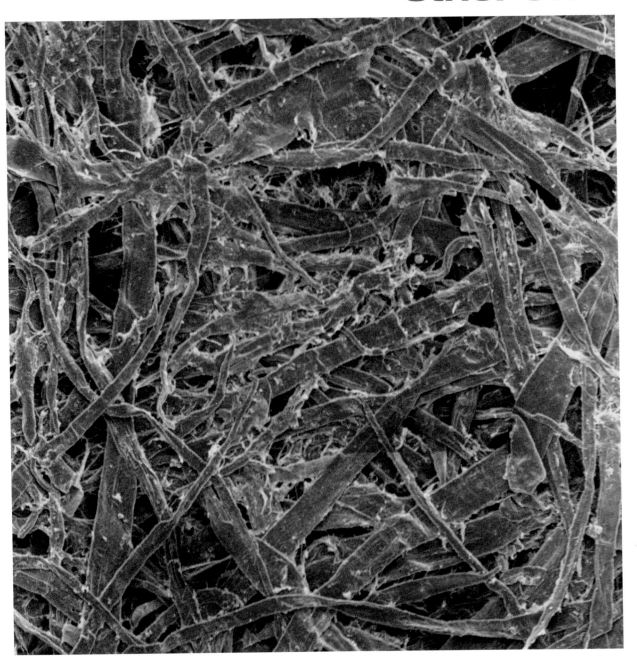

Handy while it keeps food warm, this is garbage right after the meal.

A close-up look at polystyrene foam explains why it is used so often in disposable food containers and packaging. Its outside surfaces are relatively strong and waterproof, and its core is filled with air pockets that provide lightweight strength and insulation, making it perfect for keeping hamburgers and coffee warm.

Polystyrene is a kind of plastic that has been used for more than 50 years. Scientifically, it is classified as a synthetic polymer, which means simply that it is made by combining the molecules of several compounds through a chemical reaction.

Different forms of polystyrene are made for a wide variety of uses. While its crystalline form is needed to make clear plastic cases for compact discs and audiocassettes, it can also be expanded into foam for the fast-food containers that takeout restaurants use.

To make polystyrene foam cups, manufacturers heat glassy polystyrene beads that have been loaded with pentane gas until they turn soft and white. These beads are then loosely placed into a warm mould that is the shape of a coffee cup. As the softened polystyrene beads heat, the gas expands, pressing them together against the mould to form a cup with a smooth surface made up of hexagonal cells filled with pentane gas bubbles. (Magnified 125 times.)

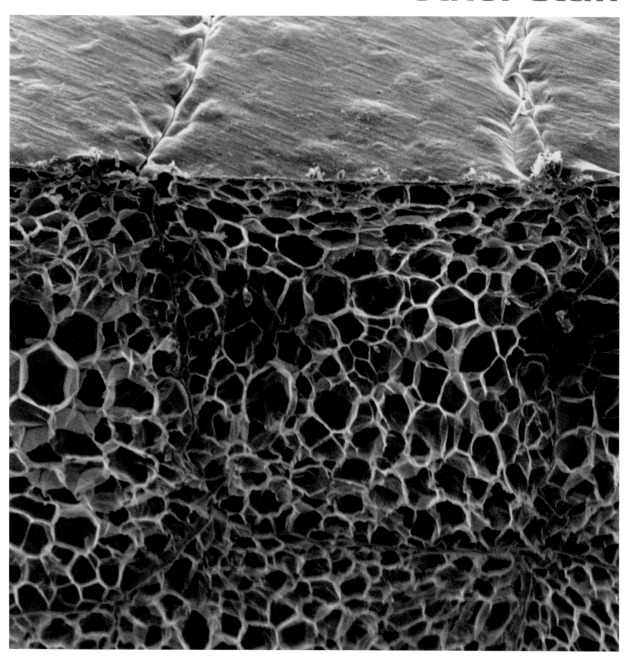

The uniform appearance of polyester cloth, facing page, gives away its synthetic origins. Engineered to perfection from petroleum by-products and chemicals, it is a plastic that is squeezed as liquid through a nozzle into smooth and continuous filaments of thread. Multiple strands are then grouped together and neatly woven into a strong and durable material.

Unlike the uniform strands of yarn found in synthetic textiles, however, cotton yarns are imperfect. A woven cotton fabric like broadcloth, above, is only as fine as the yarn that goes into it. Each strand of cotton is made from shorter ones twisted together into a thread long enough for weaving. If the cotton pieces in each strand are short, the single finished strand will be rough, giving the fabric a rough finish. (Facing page magnified 123 times. Above magnified 71 times.)

42

Opposing shapes end up clinging to one another when forced together.

A prickly encounter with the hooked bracts of a burdock seedpod during an Alpine hike in 1948 inspired Swiss mountaineer George de Mestral to create Velcro, right. For 10 long years, the inventor struggled to produce a tape of synthetic burrs — the modern-day alternative to the metal zipper. Meeting skeptics along his way, de Mestral finally found a French weaver who was able to produce cotton prototypes of the tape by hand. The soft texture of the natural fibres, however, could not withstand any repeated use, and the tape fell apart easily. In short order, de Mestral switched to a much more durable nylon thread, creating a tough fastener that held the microscopic mushroom-topped knobs embedded in a tangle of fibres.

Christened Velcro (*vel* from velvet and *cro* from crochet, which in French means little hook), the tape first appeared on the market in the mid-1950s. Forty years and millions of metres of Velcro later, de Mestral's synthetic burrs are used worldwide to close everything from running shoes, jackets and parachute packs to car upholstery and surgical openings. (Magnified 52 times.)

44

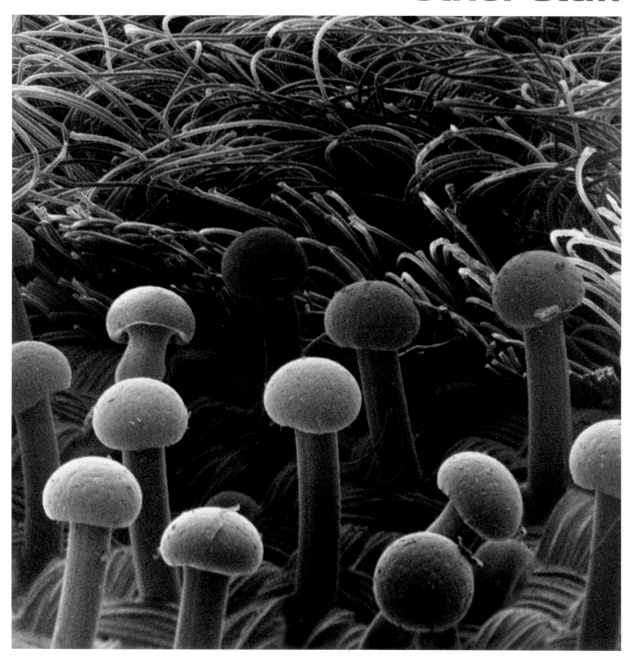

The air in a typical living room contains billions of microscopic particles that have been worn, tracked or blown into the house. Eventually, these fragments settle out of the air onto the floor and compress together into a dust ball.

Human hair, right, and threads, two of the most typical components of a dust ball, snake through the matted dirt and debris like heavy cables. Grains of sand, dirt and miniature pebbles carried in on the soles of shoes, dead and live insects (plus their offspring), spiderwebs, food particles and pet hair are other ingredients. But the most common material is flakes of skin, facing page. Humans shed billions of minute skin cells per day, a whopping 90 percent of a dust ball's raw material. Not just adding to the grit and grime in the house, human skin nourishes the large populations of tiny mites that inhabit the dust. (Below magnified 166 times. Facing page magnified 73 times.)

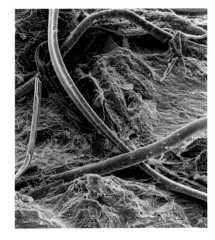

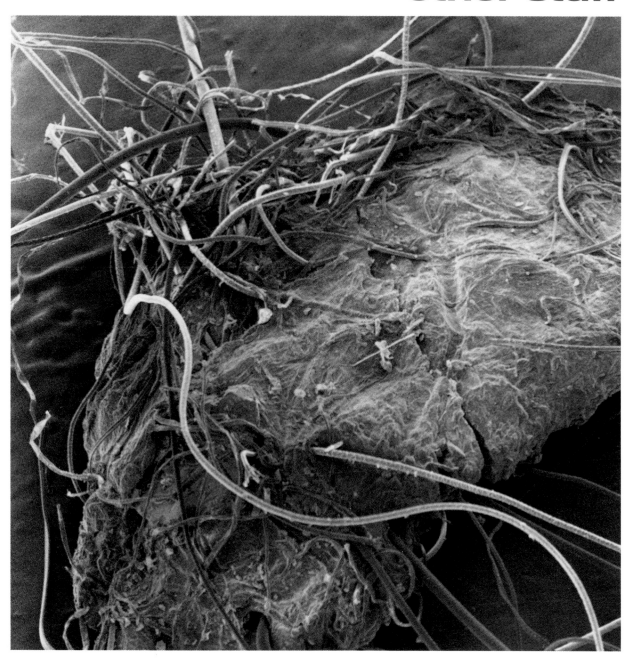

acknowledgements

This project became possible when Alexandra Smith, an electron microscopist with the University of Guelph's Department of Food Sciences, accepted the challenge of creating a series of interesting scanned images for kids. Enlisting the aid of Brenda Sun, a microscopist and recent graduate of the university's Department of Environmental Biology, Ms. Smith provided a collection of fascinating photographs using a Hitachi S-570 Scanning Electron Microscope.

Additional assistance came from the indefatigable Laurel Aziz as she researched the stories behind each of our subjects and put them into words that made sense to people who have never seen the inside of a petri dish.

And final thanks to designer Linda Menyes and the keen-eyed production duo of Charlotte DuChene and Catherine DeLury. Without their help, this book would have remained a good idea atop a pile of curious photographs.

Frank B. Edwards
July 1992